© 1995, Landoll, Inc.
Ashland, Ohio 44805
® The Landoll Apple Logo is a trademark owned by Landoll, Inc.
and is registered with the U. S. Patent and Trademark Office.
No part of this book may be reproduced or copied.
All rights reserved. Manufactured in the U.S.A.

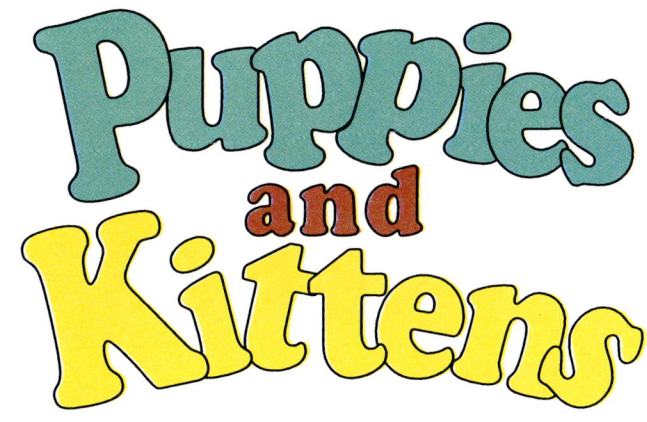

Puppies and Kittens

illustrated by Estella Hickman
written by Dandi

In the beginning, before they are born, puppies and kittens grow inside their mothers for about 2 months.

Each mother tries to find a dark, private place to give birth to her babies.

The group of babies born to Mother Cat is called a *litter*. Cats have from 2-6 kittens in a litter.

Toy breeds of dogs may have only 1 or 2 pups. Larger breeds could have litters up to 16! Since Mother only has room for 8-10, that's a problem.

Kittens are born blind and helpless. Mother Cat cleans them with her rough tongue and purrs to guide them to her milk.

Puppies are born blind and deaf. They barely have enough energy to crawl to their mother for milk.

Both cats and dogs carry their babies in their mouths to move them to safety. It may look like it hurts, but it doesn't.

In 10-14 days, puppies and kittens open their eyes.
Other senses, like hearing and smell begin to develop.

Cats can't see in the dark, but they see much better than we do in dim light.
Cat's eyes reflect light and appear to glow in the dark.

Dogs have poorer eyesight than cats. All dogs, even guide dogs, are color blind! They use smell the way we use sight.

At 3 weeks the puppies' ears open. Dogs have great hearing and can hear high frequencies humans and cats can't.

Cats rely on their amazing sense of touch. 20-30 long whiskers in rows on the side of its face help a cat sense danger.

By the third week, puppies walk instead of crawl, though they are still clumsy. They will grow up to be faster than cats.

Kittens have better balance than puppies because they have more muscles. They can turn quickly and always manage to land on their feet.

At 4 weeks, kittens like to play with their litter-mates. They know how to pull in their claws for a play-fight.

Puppies aren't able to pull in their claws. They like to play with their litter-mates too, but begin to seek people to play with.

By 6 weeks, kittens are very different from puppies. Cats walk on their toes, moving front and back legs on one side together. Only camels and giraffes walk like that!

Puppies don't have rough tongues like kittens. They stick out their tongues and pant to cool themselves off.

At 8 weeks, kittens and puppies start to look like some of these breeds:

Short-haired Cats

Manx – no tail!

Rex

Siamese

Long-haired Cats

Persian

Angora

Tabby

And at 8 weeks, puppies and kittens are old enough to want a playmate – like YOU!

Toy Dogs

Chihuahua

Shih tzu

Pomeranian

Big Dogs

St. Bernard

Collie

Dalmatian